Gavin Bassett has captured something powerful in The Assignment of Kings - a revelation that business is not separate from God's purpose but central to it. This book is a bold call to believers in the marketplace to step into their Kingdom assignment with faith, strategy, and purpose.

Through his personal journey, with its fair share of ups and downs, Gavin equips and challenges readers to see business as ministry and influence as stewardship.

For those seeking greater alignment between calling and career, this book will do just that and position you for greater impact in God's Kingdom.

> Mark Varughese,
> Founder of *Kingdomcity*
> Author of *Ready, Fire! Aim*

I am truly grateful for Gavin's book, 'The Assignment of Kings'. As follower of Jesus Christ, I was so in need of what Gavin has captured in this book. Get ready to be inspired as Gavin shares some of his personal story and uncovers how we are called to walk with God in the marketplace.

If you are in business or a leader of any kind, the lessons in this book will transform your thinking and unlock a greater opportunity for you to serve and impact, your world in a remarkable way.

> Ray Briene
> Geckoblue Australia

It's not often you get to witness a God idea, unfolding exponentially in real time. From idea to revelation, intertwined with life's experiences, 'The Assignment of Kings' will take you on a roller coaster ride, drawing from deep places to your own seeds of greatness that God has placed in you for such a time as this! Be ready to look at things differently, be ready to be inspired to step into and dream with God for that assignment. This book is positioned for a movement of Kings for the Kingdom of Heaven! Gavin has truly captured a Kairos moment with this book.

Michelle Burns
Founder of *Kingdom Doulos Prophetic Agency*

THE ASSIGNMENT OF
KINGS

GAVIN BASSETT

Published by Vivid Publishing
A division of Fontaine Publishing Group
P.O. Box 948, Fremantle
Western Australia 6959
www.vividpublishing.com.au

NATIONAL
LIBRARY
OF AUSTRALIA
A catalogue record for this
book is available from the
National Library of Australia

Cover design, artwork and layout by Rica Graphics (@ricacabrex).

Acknowledgements

Firstly, I want to acknowledge Jesus Christ my Lord and saviour, without whom I would not have been prepared for any of this.

Secondly, to my wife and family who have supported me through everything that has brought me to this point.

Thirdly, to my amazing clients who have brought a lot of this out in me without even knowing it at times.

CONTENTS

About This Book 1

My Testimony 4

My First Business 8

Queensland Bound 11

Down to Business 14

An Intro to Business Coaching 17

The Vision from God 19

I Bought a Franchise 23

The Business Degree 25

The Game Changers 27

Breakfast of Champions 30

People Are Interesting 34

Helping People 38

Going Big 42

The Rebuild 45

Million Dollar Coach 48

Collision Coming 51

A Death and a Re-Birth 54

From Nothing to Something 57

Bringing the Concept to Life 60

Building Software 63

It All Goes Wrong 66

Too Confident 69

Trying to Salvage Things 73

The Year I Never Wanted 76

Time Out 84

New Beginnings 89

Back in the Game 95

Unlocking a Gift 98

Fun and Hard Work 102

Stable 106

The Convergence 109

The Assignment of Kings 114

About This Book

The Assignment of Kings has come from my own journey through life, the marketplace and through business coupled with the realisation and revelation that God has called us to be kings and priests and has an assignment for each of us to do while we are on this planet.

While this story is about me, **this is also about you.** And my prayer is that it would provide you with revelation, inspiration and encouragement to unlock, activate and pursue your assignment.

Growing up as a pastor's kid, I had always imagined that ministry happened within the 4 walls of the Church … maybe not as clinically technical as that, but pretty close.

But my perspective on that was altered in 2003. I had been in business for myself for a couple of years and I started coaching a client who owned a Christian bookstore in Midland.

One day, after a coaching session, she gave me a book by Ed Silvoso

… "Anointed for Business" …

Reading this book completely opened my mind to a new understanding ... all of us are in ministry wherever we are and whatever we are doing.

I came to the understanding that each of us are anointed and appointed to certain vocations … mine is business ... and this is where our ministry happens.

Now, was I as intentional as I should have been, knowing this? No, unfortunately, but that would come later when I would learn about kingdom assignments.

I first came across the concept of assignment through the teachings of Dave Hodgson from Kingdom Initiatives in 2016 and it struck a chord with me.

His teachings caused me to remember that I had been anointed for business and consequently I needed to declare that my business was a kingdom business …

... a business to be used for the purpose of advancing God's Kingdom here on earth.

What I hadn't realised was that back in July 1995, God had unlocked my assignment … and since then I had been in a process of activating my assignment … to the point where I am now able to pursue my assignment with all I have.

And that is what this book is about … The Assignment of Kings … to unlock, activate and pursue your God given assignment as a kingdom builder in the marketplace … for His benefit and for His glory.

It's time to impact this planet for God through your business … and my hope and prayer is that my story plays a part in helping you.

My Testimony

When I was 6 years of age, my family started going to Church.

And shortly after this I had quite a nasty car accident on my way to school one morning, just a few days before the close of the first term of school.

A neighbour had dropped us 4 kids off. He had parked across the road from the school.

My neighbour's kid and my 3 siblings started to make their way across the road. I'm not quite sure why I was lagging (that's not my usual style).

Not wanting to be left behind, I didn't even think of looking left or looking right, instead I immediately ran out onto the road to catch up to my siblings ... and that's when I ran into the side of Mrs Colgate's car.

The car braked as I had hit it ... and I got dragged under the car ... for about 50 metres up the road until it stopped.

Ouch!!!

It turns out that if I hadn't had my school bag on my back …
I would most likely not be here today, because my bag broke
my fall, otherwise my head would have hit the road first and
that would have been that.

This was my first brush with death.

In fact, it's a miracle I can walk. The rear tyres of the car had
dragged my little legs up the road, ripping them to pieces.
So I ended up in hospital for all of the school holidays to be
put back together.

But this story is not really about my car accident, but more
about the fact that God was watching over me from a very
young age.

So, Church and God, became a part of my family, and a part
of me.

In my early teens I started to explore a relationship with
God … and shortly after I turned 15 … one Sunday evening
on the 26th of February 1984, I said yes to Jesus … I said I
really want you to be a part of my life.

I want you Jesus to lead me and direct me and help me to
become a better person.

And 40 years later (as I write this book) … I am glad I made
that decision.

You see, I have had a lot of good times in my life, thank God.

And yet, even though most don't know the full extent of the things that have happened to me … I have had a lot of extremely challenging times.

Some obvious and known ones … and some less obvious and not as well-known ones.

Some you will come to find out in this book ... others you may never come to know about.

And through the good, the bad and the other, God has been my anchor in the storms.

The firm foundation under my foot in the good times.

The one who picked me up when I fall (it seems I fall a lot).

The one who has comforted me through grief and the one who gave me hope again … when I had none.

I am so thankful for the 26th of February 1984.

Thankful that I have someone who loves me, gets me, understands me, and wants the best for me.

I am so thankful that I have God in my life.

If you're looking for a perfect Christian, please look somewhere else …

I am a work in progress that is loved by God and grateful for that.

Here's the thing, God saved me from potential death at the age of 6

… and God saved me forever at the age of 15, my name is eternally written in the Lamb's book of life.

Why? Because God created me on purpose for a purpose. He had an assignment for me to fulfill on this planet to advance His Kingdom here on earth … I just had to say yes!

My First Business

The 28th of November 2024 marked 23 years since I purchased an Action International Business Coaching Franchise (now known as ActionCoach).

In that time, I have had many iterations of a coaching, mentoring, training and education business.

Including creating our own software for a business education platform, with a business partner (Rueben).

So, a lot had happened in those 23 years, that's for sure.

But my business journey didn't start there. My entrepreneurial journey started back in 1982, when I was just 13 years of age.

And it was thanks to Jack Mavor, an amazing man. I contracted my services to him every Saturday.

He would pay me in money and in knowledge ... which was cool.

From there I branched out with my own gardening and cleaning business.

Roping mates into my escapades, gardening, and cleaning around the neighbourhood.

At 16, I became a commission only newspaper sales boy.

My area was the light industrial business precinct, which opened my eyes up to the variety of businesses out there.

I made more money from tips than I did from selling papers.

In that period, I came to understand that relationships were more important than the product.

I looked after my customers, showed an interest in their day and my customers loved me and tipped me handsomely.

The newspaper was simply a bi-product.

I finished high school in 1986, failing English, so no University for me.

And this changed the course of my life, because until then, I had my heart set on becoming a marine biologist.

I had it all worked out, I was moving to Queensland, and the ocean was going to be my workplace.

But this was not to be however!

So, in 1987 I joined the Westpac bank … why? Because my brother worked there.

To be honest, I did have 2 offers on the table from two different banks at the time, Westpac wanted me to start a month later than the other bank, and this suited me better, because I had a surf trip lined up that I was keen to go on.

Banking was a good fit for me ... I loved numbers and money ... what more did I need to think about.

And it was here that I crafted my business skills even further. Westpac was great at training people. Not just training you to do your job, but to lead and to manage.

So, my training in managing and leading had begun. And within 2 years ... something extraordinary occurred ... maybe even supernatural.

Queensland Bound

In 1988 I booked a trip to Brisbane to go to the World Expo.

Who knows why, but that's what I did.

But 3 weeks before I was due to head off, I had my first little set back as an adult.

On the 8th of August 1988 I had a rostered day off and had headed to the beach for a surf.

During my time out in the water, 3 blokes decided they would steal my car and go for an extreme joy ride, destroying my car engine.

As all my savings were earmarked for my Queensland trip, Dad came to the rescue with the finances for a reconditioned engine (and of course I paid him back, later).

So, I packed my bags and my surfboard, and I was off for a month.

I had to fly to Sydney first, and while I was waiting in the airport reading a book, a bloke opposite me cleared his throat several times to get my attention.

I looked at the bloke, then having a realisation, looked at the back of my book, wide eyed now.

I then look at the bloke again, because my initial realisation turned out to be true, he was the author of the book.

I know right!

Crazy sauce!!

We got talking and he asked me what I do. I told him that I'm in banking.

He then says, yeah but what do you want to do with your life? This is such a great question to ask a young person!!!

I was 19 at the time … but I answered him pretty quickly. I'm going to own my own business one day.

He asks, doing what?

I don't really know, I say, with a bit of a wry smile.

He said, "Can I offer you some advice"? I'm like heck yeah, you've written a book, you must know some things!

He then tells me I should navigate my career in the bank into business banking.

And I should build up my knowledge base about business from people in business.

Yep, the bank's clients.

Don't just lend them money ... find out about them.

How they do business, why they do it that way, what works for them, what doesn't.

A chance meeting with Dr Noel Vose?

I think not! More like a divine appointment.

Now here's the thing ... it's one thing to be given advice ... but another thing to do something with that advice ... so what would happen if I implemented what he advised me to do?

Down to Business

Well, I took up Dr Noel's advice and by 1990 I had my first taste of dealing with business owners in the bank.

As my career took off, I got deeper and deeper into the commercial banking side of the bank.

Having many great mentors along the way.

People like Ben Marini, John Vincent, and Pat Maher … again, I don't think this was by chance. People who not only knew their stuff, but they also knew how to mentor a young man like me.

In 1997 I was appointed as one of the Credit Managers in commercial banking, which I really enjoyed and was able to learn so much more practically about business and finances.

And life is interesting with its twists and turns, because I had applied for a number of jobs as a relationship manager, so that I could get as close to the coal face as possible.

Only to be pipped at the post by someone else each time I applied.

But one day, one of my friends made the brave move to join another bank.

And jokingly, as he was leaving, I said "don't forget me, Michael" (it really was a joke).

Well, less than 6 months later he called me.

"Hey, Gav, there's a job going at St.George as a Relationship Manager and I reckon you should go for it".

And that's what I did … updated my resume from almost 12 years earlier and went for it.

Needless to say, I got the job and a 40% pay rise. Yep, not a typo … hahahaha.

So, in October 1998 I entered a domain which was very different to where I had been.

I started out with a small portfolio of about $40 Million and just me.

And by the time I left 3 years later, it was around $80 Million, and I had 2 staff.

Several cool things happened in that 3 years at St.George. Firstly, I was given a lot of autonomy to run it how I wanted to.

So, I ran it like a small business, with customer service being my leading weapon.

I learnt as much as I could off every business owner I looked after.

I got to know their businesses and how and why they did things intimately.

I had a ridiculous variety of businesses, from law firms, to vineyards, to dotcoms, to backpackers to pubs, to retails shops … and anything in between.

I gave my staff responsibility over parts of the portfolio.

And one day when I was feeling very comfortable with my lot in life.

Two blokes walked into my office to borrow some money.

And what happened next changed my life forever …

An Intro to Business Coaching

So, these two blokes wanted to borrow some money, and my first question was: how much do you want and what do you want it for?

They wanted a significant sum of money for a property deal (that's all I can say).

I asked, what do you blokes do?

They said, we own a Master Franchise of a Business Coaching company.

I said, "a what"????

What is this business coaching?

Red flags going up everywhere for me …

Now, you need to understand, as a lender, I always started from NO and worked my way to a yes (maybe).

Yep, sad but true.

And this approach made me do my due diligence exceedingly well.

Which ultimately was good for me and my customers (and the bank).

Anyways, I did my due diligence … extra due diligence this time.

And when I had finished doing my due diligence, I was thinking, hmmm, I want to buy one of these business coaching franchises

So, I go home to the wifey, as I had done with 50 other hair brained ideas before (a little exaggeration my wife says, maybe it was 12).

And something strange happened this time.

You see, she had said NO deal to everything before this.

But this time … She says, I reckon that this business coaching thing is you all over.

Ooooooooo … here we go.

Before I go on … let me take you back to 1995. It's important … and explains a lot about what happens in this story …

The Vision from God

You may want to grab a coffee.

In 1995 I went to a Church conference in Sydney.

My wife and I had driven across from Perth to stay with my brother and sister-in-law, who were living in Sydney at the time. A three and a half day drive!

I came to this conference hungry for God to do something in my life. So, every day before the conference I would get on my knees and pray for about an hour or so.

But this didn't just happen ... this was a process of hunger building over time.

Let me explain.

Exactly one year earlier, my wife and I had flown across the Hillsong Conference. This was the first time we had been to anything like this.

For a little more context, we had largely been brought up in a Baptist Church setting ... not that there is anything wrong with that. However, the move of the Holy Spirit was not really something we had fully experienced.

And yet here we were in a conference that was literally demanding the presence of the Holy Spirit ... and I was very attracted to that notion.

We were sitting a long way back from the stage ... but I wanted what they were talking about.

I mean I really wanted the whole presence of the Holy Spirit ... and without anyone laying hands on me, in amoment of what I can only describe as the touch of God, I was baptised in the Holy Spirt and started speaking intongues (the holy language of heaven).

This was a defining moment ... a moment that created a hunger for God like I had not had before.

Now I'm not saying any of this to impress you, but to explain something and to impress upon you the power of God and what happens when you establish a hunger for him.

And so, with that hunger that had built up, at that conference in 1995, I wanted to know from God (not from man), what do you have in store for me?

What do you want me to do with my life, God? How may I be of service to you? These were my questions.

I know that this may not make sense to some, but it made sense to me then, and even more so now.

Anyways, after the first day after pouring my heart and soul out to God ... I hear NOTHING!

So, I went back the next day and did it all over again.

Curiously, I heard nothing again.

I know right ... what is going on?? I'm hungry to know the answers to my questions, where are you God?

So, I go back the third day, with the same level of earnestness as the previous two days (maybe even more) ... and oh my word!!!

I have never seen anything like this before, or since.

It was like someone had a projector on a sheet, that's the best way I can describe it. You know, like movie night in the backyard in the seventies where mum had pegged a sheet to the clothes line and Dad had his movie projector going.

Right in front of my eyes, I see what looks like a movie of me, but it's in the future.

I am on a stage in front of hundreds of business people. And I'm teaching them about business.

I think to myself, REALLY? ME? Ummmm, this 26 year old?? What do I know? How could I teach?

Then I hear the Lord say, "this is not now, but get ready for the future, you will know it when you see it".

I got the distinct impression it would be 5-6 years into the future.

So, when I got home, I shared this with my Pastor, who happened to be my Dad.

Then I asked him, "what do you reckon"?

He says to me … I can see you doing that! And I'm like, well that just got real!

So, when those 2 blokes came into my office in late 2001.

And I had finished doing my due diligence.

Then my wife said, yep that's you all over.

And I started to remember 1995 … and started wondering whether this opportunity that had literally walked through my door … was THE OPPORTUNITY.

I Bought a Franchise

So I said to God, "hey Lord, if this is it, then I'm going to put my house on the market, so I can fund this purchase".

And, "if this is from you and what you want … then the house has to sell in 7 days for X dollars".

I know, great man of faith etc etc … hahahaha. But God is gracious and good …

And the house sells for the exact amount and in 7 days.

So, I go ahead and buy the franchise, with a little family help. And I headed off to Queensland for 10 days of intensive training. I mean really intensive.

Now I was pretty fortunate that when I left the bank, my boss agreed to allow me to market to my past clients.

So, as soon as I got back from training, that's exactly what I did.

Straight on the phone, setting up meetings.

And before Christmas hit, I had 3 clients.

I helped my first client make an extra $42,000 in profits within 11 weeks.

Now I must admit, I was a bit full on back then.

And I was throwing everything I had at those first few clients.

I pretty much overwhelmed them to exploding their minds, eeeek

… and consequently, they didn't last long because of that.

But praise be to God, I work this out pretty quickly. And my future clients got the benefit of my learnings. Then I started marketing to people I didn't know at all. People wanted to know my qualifications.

Which was interesting for a bloke that had failed high school.

Yes, I had a heap of experience working with businesses in my near on 15 years in the bank.

But something I didn't lead with … was my degree!

Maybe I thought it was a bit too much like puffing your chest out or something, which wasn't really how I rolled.

Yet, it turned out this "degree" was important.

But how did a guy that failed high school get a business degree …

The Business Degree

Here's a quick jump back in time.

Back in my banking days when I had just turned 20.

I had the usual annual review with HR and I was told, "Son, if you want to climb the corporate ladder, it's best if you get a degree".

Ummmm … I failed High School.

Well then, you should go to night school and re-sit your leaving exams.

So that's what I did in 1989 … a whole year of night school.

Two nights a week, every week, while working full time. And I managed to pass with flying colours and got the score I needed to get into Uni.

So, I did a double degree in business, majoring in Finance and Management.

I continued to work full time and did my university studies at night, getting an education and earning money.

Somewhere in amongst climbing the corporate ladder and going to university ... I got married to the most amazing woman, we had our first son and then I graduated with a double degree in business.

For some reason the degree not only unlocked doors in the bank. It also unlocked doors in the business world.

Yet the degree was not the shining light in what happened next.

The Game Changers

What is interesting in life and in business … is moments.

Moments when someone comes into your life.

Like a Jack Mavor, or Dr Vose.

I call them "Game Changer" people.

Earlier on in my business days, I used to send out direct mail to complete strangers. Yep, I was that guy.

My letter had a lollypop attached to it.

This helped break the ice when calling people, which is pretty handy, when you have a fear of speaking to people you don't know.

Yep, that's me … and still me. I know right!

Anyways, the first game changer clients I had were this amazing couple … Mick and Beth Fitzpatrick.

What I discovered with them was the power of dreams.

Not any dreams … dreams that drive you to take action no matter what.

See business is cool and fun.

But cooler and more fun when you're going after a dream.

That moment when you realise your business can serve you and deliver your dreams.

And as Brian Tracy is famous for saying … "without a why, I won't even try".

Now Mick and Beth had a dream of owning a twin hull cat, so that they could sail around the world in it.

It was something they had hoped for and wanted for a very long time.

But it seemed out of reach, because when we first started working together, their business had them trapped.

Like hamsters on a wheel.

In our first few meetings we uncovered their dream.

And together we created a plan to make their dream both possible and achievable.

Then we went for it … like a partnership.

I enjoyed every moment of working with them. They were coachable and they were great students.

They put the work in and then some, taking action week in week out.

And 13 months later, they had their business completely under control.

Which I have discovered over many years of doing this, that this short time frame is highly unusual.

Yet here they were under control and with time and money freedom to boot.

This then opened up other opportunities.

I got to be part of their story … and they got to be part of mine.

This cemented something for me … a massive key to business success is clarity on your dreams.

And the next game changer was about to happen too …

Breakfast of Champions

The other moments in life and business are decisions.

Not just decisions made, but decisions carried out.

One of my mentors Keith J Cunningham has a saying … the idea is worth 1% … the execution of the idea is worth 99%.

People make all kinds of decisions, but nothing happens until they act on those decisions.

In early 2002, I wasn't making all the sales I could. And because I'm an innovator by nature, I had an idea.

Brad Sugars the founder of ActionCOACH had run a 2 day workshop back in the day.

It was called "The Competitive Edge" … I had it on video and on audio tape.

Now some of the franchisees in NZ, Bruce Taylor was one of them, I think, had this group coaching idea.

When I heard about it, I immediately went to The Competitive Edge series I had.

And I thought, hey, if I carve that up into chunks, then deliver it fortnight by fortnight, what would that look like?

Well, it ended up being 7 sessions over 2 and half months.

And I made it very affordable for small businesses to invest in themselves.

Around about the same time, I had the opportunity to present at a local business breakfast.

It was called **Breakfast of Champions**. And I used the opportunity to launch my first Group Coaching program.

I signed up 4 businesses … and away I went.

Now to get ready to present these group coaching workshops … I must have listened to and watched those cassettes and videos at least 30 times (that's like 540 hours).

I had the content etched into my mind, almost word for word.

Now I have always had an inner need to do things with excellence

… possibly borderline perfectionism … eeeek.

And they say practise makes perfect right? So I did all I could to deliver these workshops with excellence.

One of the businesses that attended my first Group Coaching program, was Brendan Carlin from Prestige Lock Services (which he owned at the time).

Brendan was a go getter and a challenger.

He didn't just accept things straight off the bat.

He questioned things (not everything, but almost everything) and he kept me on my toes.

I think that's a good thing. Not always comfortable, but good, because it keeps you sharp.

After the Group Coaching Program finished, he continued on in my 1-2-1 coaching program.

We had a lot of fun together growing his business.

During the time we worked together, it became almost impossible to hire qualified tradies.

So, Brendan came up with the idea of hiring 2 apprentices at the same time.

Healthy competition for each other … and more hands making light work.

Sometimes in business you need someone to bounce the idea off.

To help you work through the pros and cons and then to back you and encourage you to do it.

That's where progress happens, and I've had countless opportunities to do just that with clients over the years.

And when you are working with growing businesses … it causes you to grow too.

Yet growth rarely comes without challenges, whether they be inside the business or outside the business.

As I was about to find out!

People Are Interesting

In the July of that year, I decided to go to the Hillsong Conference in Sydney with my Dad.

I had been a number of times before and it was a great time for both personal growth and spiritual growth.

A few weeks before I left to go on this trip, I had got into my car one morning with my son Connor (then 5) and I noticed that the interior light cover and bulb were on the floor of the car.

So, what did I do? I immediately asked my son if he had been playing around with said light in Daddy's Jeep?

He said, 'no Dad with a shake of his head' ... he has always been an honest lad, so of course I believed him.

And so, I just put it down to an oddity of life ... and I put it all back together and kind of forgot about this incident.

Well, it turns out there was something afoot that I would later discover.

One stormy night, while I was at the conference in Sydney,

three young blokes decided that they would take my Jeep on an ATM heist.

Clearly, they had attempted this once before but had been disturbed, hence the interior light issue I had come across earlier.

Needless to say, while they succeeded in taking my Jeep, they failed in their endeavours of pulling an ATM out of the wall in downtown Kwinana.

So, their next best plan was to take my Jeep slightly off road, roll it and then burn it to a shell.

And as inconvenient as it was that they had taken my Jeep … more inconvenience was to come.

Somehow, between buying the Jeep 2.5 years earlier and this point in time of having it stolen, there was now a deficit between the insurance value of my Jeep and the outstanding loan.

Which meant I now no longer had a vehicle, but I had a debt …

and with a business only 7 months old, I had no way of getting finance for another vehicle.

This is when I discovered that people are interesting (possibly shallow).

When I got back from that conference, I was having to go out and about for business in my wife's 3 door Hyundai Excel.

Not exactly the business vehicle that says, hey, I'm a success and I know what I'm doing ... sign up for my coaching program ... as it turns out.

My sales strike rate had been reasonably good until then, but went down dramatically to a strike rate of 1/10 at best.

Worse than that, an existing client (who ran a high-end business) saw me leave one day in my wife's car ... and shortly after sent me an email stating they no longer required my services!

This was odd, as we had been getting some outstanding results together and were getting along quite well, so I thought (hmmmm).

The reason I say people are interesting, me included, is because quite often we judge others based on looks and appearance, rather than on substance and results.

Even though we were all taught in school, don't judge a book by its cover! Yet that is exactly what we do.

So, I was left to find a way of showing people what they wanted to see, so that I could give them what they needed.

Not exactly the best thing in life, but sometimes you just have to be shrewd ... yet there are hidden consequences to this.

None of this stopped me from wanting to help people, which led to what happened next …

Helping People

Towards the end of 2002, I bought another business, no money down.

And also started a third business.

Well of course I did … I was an entrepreneur!

And possibly quite stupid … hahahahaha.

I even got a franchise award for "Entrepreneurial Spirit" … not all awards are a help, just saying.

Anyways … I was smart enough to get out of those 2 other businesses by June 2003.

Which enabled me to concentrate on my coaching business, and so in 2003, I employed my first employee. Alexander Patterson.

She ran my marketing for me.

She talked to all the prospects for me. And all I had to do was sell.

We sat down together one day and mapped out the sales process.

Which became known as the 13 Step Sales Process throughout the franchise, ActionCOACH.

A very innovative name of course ... it had 13 steps hehehehe.

Surprisingly it became quite catchy within the franchise group I was part of.

Now I'm not saying I created the process, but I did map it out and systemise it.

And we followed that system to a tee. And my little business grew and grew. Hitting milestone after milestone.

I was running radio ads and advertising in the local newspaper ... it was go, go, go.

I was running seminars and group coaching programs. I had my 1-2-1 clients.

I was the treasurer of the Rockingham Chamber of Commerce.

And then I made a decision to team up with another franchisee and move my office to Burswood in early 2004.

I was still running a group coaching program in Rockingham, and this is where I met the delightful Colin and Pauline Bright.

They graduated from Group Coaching to the 1-2-1 coaching program.

And we did some amazing things together.

Pauline will feature again in my story … another game changer!

In my first few years as a coach, I was devouring books and audio books, because learning leads to earning.

I would read at least one book every week.

I did a lot of road travelling back then and so my mentors in the car were: Jim Rohn, Zig Ziglar, Tom Hopkins, Tony Robbins, Steven Covey, and Brian Tracy, to name a few.

Zig Ziglar had a saying … if you help enough people get what they want, you will get everything you want.

I said okay Zig, let me test that out.

Within our franchise group we had a forum, where we could ask questions and get support from each other.

I figured I would try and help as many people as I could, knowing that it would sharpen my skills and knowledge too.

A win: win for everyone.

My business continued to grow.

And at the 2004 Global Franchise conference that year, I was awarded Global Team Player of the Year.

I wasn't expecting that, but I received it gladly.

And to top it off, I also won Coach of the Year for WA.

Things were looking good.

Shortly after this, another franchisee from WA had a conversation with me ... And this conversation would alter everything I had been doing.

Going Big

After the 2004 Global Conference one of the franchisees approached me and 2 other franchisees with a proposition.

Let's start a company and fold all our franchises into that company. Then let's start bringing on new franchisees into this company.

The idea had BIG appeal to me, and I wasn't that content in the office sharing arrangement I was in at that time.

So, over the course of a few months, we talked, we strategized, and we got to know each other a little more.

This was an intentional process designed to see if we could make this work together.

By the end of November 2004, we had agreed we could make this work.

And 4 little businesses amalgamated into one company with 4 franchises, turning over about $750K per annum … unheard of in our space at that moment in time.

We quickly brought on a marketing person and another franchisee

… and we were away.

We had vision, we had passion, we had energy … we thought that we were unstoppable (and that can be good and that can be bad).

We leased a large office in East Perth, took up the entire top floor … no expenses were being spared.

We had a number of go-getter clients who had either got to a place where their business worked without them, or their partner was able to handle it without them.

So, we started talking to some of these clients about becoming coaches.

One of these go-getters was Pauline Bright … an amazing woman with a mind and heart for business.

Our Firm quickly became 10 coaches … we thought we were super stars (maybe we were, maybe we weren't).

And at the Australian Franchise Conference in Melbourne in 2005, we devised a cunning plan (or at least we thought we did).

We wanted to do a deal to buy some franchises in bulk at a better rate.

Unbeknown to us, the Franchisor already had that idea.

So, 2 of us had a meeting with one of the Franchisors and we were told by our partners, just hear the deal, don't do the deal.

Ummm, yeah ... we did the deal ... an option to buy franchises in bundles ... our option was for 20 all up ... gulp.

So, when we got back to Perth, we got busy.

We increased our marketing team, expanding it to 5, plus an intern. We started running seminars every week.

We were making sales hand over fist. We were filling group coaching courses.

We were filling our coaches up with 1-2-1 clients.

And by the time the 2006 Global Conference came around ... we thought we were almost untouchable.

At the Global Franchise Conference, we pretty much cleaned up, winning countless awards.

Including winning Global Firm of the Year. It was almost mind-boggling.

But no-one is untouchable, as we were soon to find out.

The Rebuild

Two of our gun coaches, Pauline and Peter, bought some franchises off us and set up shop down south in Mandurah.

They thought this was good and we thought this was good.

For us this was the prototype of what we were going to do on a large scale.

And as we headed into 2007, we continued to grow. We continued to add coaches to our Firm.

We were turning over $250-300K every month … but this is where things got shaky.

In July/August that year, one of our partners called it a day … and she had been a huge driving force with our vision.

We paid her out, but the loss of her drive was noticeable.

And in late 2007 I made some pretty bad decisions … without my usual due diligence or being true to myself … one would come and bite me hard in 2016 (I just didn't know it then).

So we rolled into 2008 … and from the outside things probably looked pretty peachy.

In fact, over that period the revenue was still good, and we continued to collect award after award.

Including personally receiving a 40 under 40 Award … I just scraped in at the age of 39 and a bit.

But on the inside of our business, there was a lot of turmoil.

Things were slowly falling apart … and we couldn't seem to put things back together.

We made some tough decisions and also some dumb decisions.

Then another one of our business partners called it a day, having moved to the east coast of Australia.

Which saw us start selling off parts of the business to coaches within our business who were keen.

Consequently, our team of 23+ (at its peak), became a team of 3 by early 2009.

And somehow, we were carrying a $500K debt in the wash up … So, it was time to re-charge, reset and go forward in a new way.

Over the 2007 and 2008 period, I had only been working with a couple of clients, because I was largely coaching the team and presenting.

And so, I had to rebuild my client base.

We moved to a smaller office across the street.

I reset my sights on qualifying at the highest levels within our franchise group.

First Diamond level … then Millionaire level.

T. Harv Eker once said, "your inner world controls your outer world".

So, I went to work on my inner world, who I was, and who I said I was and what I was capable of.

With a lot of work, I could clearly see my path forward.

In fact, I was able to get myself into a state of knowing exactly what it felt like to arrive (even though I had not physically arrived yet).

The mind is a powerful unit, and the key is to harness it.

And harnessing my mind and taking the right actions at the right time, led to what happened next.

Million Dollar Coach

What happened next is arguably some of my greatest years in business.

Between the 3 of us in the "new" business ... we were turning over 40-50% of what 23+ had been. Not a bad effort.

We had regular seminars going on.

We had FULL group coaching programs.

I raced to Diamond level and got a fancy pen with a diamond in it

… whoot whoot.

I was coaching some amazing people, like Walter Ferrari, Adam Garnaut, James Taylor, Peter Spark, Michael Rosario, to name a few.

My clients were getting great results ... and I was getting great results and by May 2010, I achieved the Millionaire Coach level.

And if my information is correct, two of us achieved that at the same time … a first ever within ActionCOACH … yep, looking at you Bruza Campbell.

We paid off the debt we had within 18 months (which turned out to be a good thing for the business and a bad thing for me personally, I would find that out later).

Once again, I was living in that feeling of "unstoppable".

I was building a stellar class of clientele … a true community of like- minded business people.

Adding clients like Helen Golisano, Trevor Hughes, Richard Crommelin, and Ruth Hatherley to name a few …

Then God came calling in 2011 … it's time to go out on your own again.

Not what I wanted to hear … so I ignored that, (I know right).

God is very persistent … so in the end I had to have the tough conversation with my business partner, Rueben Taylor, to wrap up that part of journey.

And while I went out on my own, we still held our quarterly planning sessions together.

And also, the epic workshop of all time "Vision Builders" … a 4 day weekend in Bali in 2012 with our top clients.

Business was good … almost in cruise control, and a lot of fun.

A group of clients started coming to the Business Excellence Forum with me, which was held on the east coast of Australia.

There were awards to go for ... and we did that.

But in March 2014, we came away empty handed. Not one of us were happy about that.

And this was the start of an additional service to my top clients - the Platinum Partnership.

A lunch/workshop, every month, in addition to whatever coaching program this group of clients was on.

6 businesses would meet with me in a group designed to get even better results.

There was rigour, there was learning, there was challenge.

An amazing group of people, with some amazing businesses. And the next year we cleaned up, winning a number of awards.

But something else happened in 2014, which ended up having quite the impact on my business, something I did not see coming.

Collision Coming

2014 was a turning point in my business and in my life.

There was a collision coming, I just didn't know it. They say hindsight is a wonderful thing, which is true.

And while not everything that happens to you in life is your fault, a lot is.

So, I own 100% of what was building in the background ... because 3 things came down to a lack of due process by me.

A decision to buy a property in 2007 that I shouldn't have.

A decision in 2009-2011 to pay off business debt way too fast without the proper tax structures in place for me personally.

And then the 3rd piece to the puzzle ... distraction.

I just didn't know it was distraction at the time.

I thought it was the right thing and a good thing.

But for those who know, a good thing is not always a God thing ... which you either find out through due process beforehand, or you find out the hard way later, because of a lack of due process.

Mine was the latter … yay!!!

Some of this is not my entire story to tell … so I will be a little guarded on the detail.

Needless to say, I made the choice to go into pastoral ministry inside the 4-walls of the Church I was attending at the time, without any of us doing our spiritual due diligence.

I stepped into a role as a Campus Pastor of one of the campuses of the Church and also took on the role as the Connect Group Pastor for the Church as a whole.

Neither of these were necessarily full-time roles. However, there is a saying … you cannot serve 2 masters. And this turned out to be completely true.

Even though I continued to provide a high standard of service to my clients in my business.

I had zero focus on marketing or sales to grow my business … and consequently my business started to decline.

And this was because I was convinced by myself and some others, that I would end up in full-time ministry in the Church.

Which is odd that I would have thought that … given the calling on my life to go into business (and no calling to full-time ministry inside the Church).

And so, in the business I only did what I had to do, in order to maintain what I had.

But business is like a living organism … it is not one to be maintained … it is one to be grown and nurtured.

One of my mentors used to say, "in business if you're not growing, your dying".

But at the time, that statement did not occur to me, yet it was becoming my reality.

And it was happening little by little … and was hard to notice, because I was not paying attention to this side of the business.

An area I had always paid firm attention to.

Now by the standard for most, 2014 wasn't too bad on paper … but the collision was coming whether I liked it or not.

A Death and a Re-Birth

It wasn't until mid to late 2015 that I started to realise that I was on a slippery slope going down with not much to grip on to.

I did what I could to maintain it.

But it seemed that nothing that I did was working now … and this what not something I was personally used to.

Yet … in amongst all that, my clients were getting outstanding results.

We cleaned up at the annual awards.

The entire Platinum Partnership crew and I went to Bali in the October for 3 days of UNLOCKED with Jonathan McDonald.

And all of us came away from that experience with business ideas and concepts to solve real problems out there in the marketplace.

Unfortunately, that didn't help my current situation … but it did give me some hope of what could be next.

This is where the online business education platform Biznostics was birthed … in concept at least.

It was very clear in my mind what it needed to look like and how it would help small business owners get the fundamentals in place to help make running their business easier.

I shared my concept with my previous business partner, Rueben Taylor … and it turned out he had a very similar concept.

So, we agreed to mastermind this together and see where it went.

In the meantime, I was still trying all kinds of things to unwind the mess I had created for myself through those 3 poor decisions in my own business and life.

But it all seemed too little, too late.

There needed to be drastic changes … and drastic changes there were.

I was seeking the Lord as to what was going on and what I needed to do.

Days went past. Weeks went past … and then in a moment I heard him say, "when did I call you away from business?"

I'm not sure if you've ever had one of those absolute gulp moments, but that was definitely one for me.

So, I resigned my pastoral roles at the Church … as I was

crystal clear that the business marketplace was where I needed to be.

And because of where things were at financially, I had to liquidate my company and hand in my franchise over to the franchisor and all my clients were transferred into Rueben's franchise.

Then came my lifeline, I got to work with Rueben in his Franchise, with my crew of clients ... and did I have to swallow some humble pie. Ummmm YEP!

But out of the ashes we had started the process of taking a raw idea of Biznostics ... from a concept ... to life.

From Nothing to Something

So, 2016 became a crazy mixed-up year … no longer being a franchisee … selling my home for a massive loss.

And exchanging my amazing car and imac computer to make a $400,000 problem go away (who woulda thunk you could do that).

Being in a tech start-up?!? (I wouldn't have thought that in my wildest imagination … and my imagination is wild) … and still getting to coach my A-team of clients.

There was a lot to manage … so much emotion, so much anxiety, so much shame, and also so much excitement ... all rolled into one.

Quite a strange combination really …

It was a year I would not have survived if not for God, my wife and Rueben … in that order.

I distinctly remember my wife saying, "honey, none of this stuff matters that much, we have each other, and we have God".

And it turns out, that was something I needed to hear.

2016 was a year that I learnt family and friends were way more important than things and stuff … and my whole concept of true success changed.

True success is the people you can count on … the "real" relationships you have.

Not my assets or my cashflow … and while these things are nice, and I really do enjoy them, oh yes, I do … at the end of the day … I could always go back to drawing board and make more.

So, that's what I started to do … with Rueben … the birth of Biznostics.

The interesting thing in all that had gone down for me, were the lessons and the experiences.

I somehow had so much more empathy for things I saw business owners going through, that I didn't have before.

I had a much better understanding of what was going on and I had the strategies and tactics of how to get out of what was going on.

No experience should ever be wasted … and I wasn't about to waste all this.

It seemed the more I went through, the more I could help others.

Now, I'm not suggesting anyone should go about doing dumb things, just to get those experiences … Hahahaha.

But I am saying they are in fact priceless, valuable, and extremely useful.

So, licking my wounds, and with crazy tenacity, I kept moving … after all, we had a concept to birth.

In mid-2016, we decided to do one of Roger Hamilton's entrepreneurs bootcamps in Bali … 15 days of getting it out of our heads onto paper.

And 15 days of surfing Keramas … AWESOME!!!

We fleshed this thing out, got clarity on what we wanted to build and did a lot of research.

By the time we left Bali, we had a clear action plan … and I had a meniscus tear in my left knee (not part of any plan) … ouch!

As soon as we got back from Bali, we joined the Founder Institute program for tech start-ups … and really started to build out the first iteration of Biznostics … our MVP – Minimum Viable Product.

We seemed to be in the right place and the right space to get this thing off the ground.

Bringing the Concept to Life

Every week at the Founders Institute we were learning about the tech space ... building our concept out more ... pitching our business every week to mentors and investors, and this was just to stay in the game.

Each week, at least one business wouldn't make the cut and that was the end of the road in the program for them.

So, it was a little stressful week in week out trying to prove that your business concept was worthy enough to stay in the program.

After maybe 12-13 weeks (it may have been 16 weeks), finally, we had something, now it wasn't pretty, but it was functional ... well sort of.

Biznostics was held together with google sheets, google docs, sticky tape, and paperclips ... but it was launched.

At the end of the program the top 3 businesses got to do a pitch off to a panel of experts to see who was best in class, so to speak.

And Biznostics was acknowledged as one of the top 2 performers of the cohort … which won us a trip to Silicon Valley to mix it up with the big boys.

So, in May 2017 we went off to the US of A to a meet up with the other cohort winners from around the world for a 3-day Master Class with the "Experts in the Industry".

Let's just say, we met a lot of people … and at best, they showed some marginal interest in what we had … but no one was lining up to invest to help us take over the world.

With that said, we learnt a lot … and came back home and started building version 1 of our software … we believed … and for that moment in time, that was enough.

So, we were coaching one week and building our software the other week.

We were testing what we had with small business owners … getting feedback and more importantly, helping them get results for their businesses.

Now it was time to go out there and get some paying clients … could we find people who would pay to use our online business education platform?

The simple answer was, yes, we could … with a however …

… we discovered that people left to their own devices (yes even so- called motivated business owners) … have good intentions.

Intentions, however, rarely lead to action … and it is action that leads to results.

Houston, we had a problem.

And the problem was that our concept of 24/7 access to learn how to run and build your business at your pace … whenever it suits you.

Well, let's just say, without accountability and without stickiness (as they say in the tech world) … and in the absence of true gamification … we had to adapt.

So, we packaged the first version of the platform with a short call each week … and purposely kept the pricepoint low and super affordable.

All this with the aim to get it back to our original concept … at some point in the future.

We now had paying clients.

We were now getting real time feedback … which was thanks to the weekly calls.

But we were a long way from what we had in mind.

It was time to build version 2 … so that is what we looked to do next.

Building Software

We had in mind exactly what we wanted to create - true.

We thought we had done enough product market fit testing. This was probably not true.

So, we created our product specification, complete with wireframes and it was time to see who could build the front end of the diagnostic tool for Biznostics.

We spoke with 3 software developers, all with various skillsets.

Some could do it all locally in Australia, some would outsource overseas.

The quotes came in, ranging from $50,000 to $600,000. Quite a range, mind-blowing really.

We wanted it built in Australia, so we chose a Sydney based firm … Honed … and the project began.

Honed were great to deal with.

They got where we were coming from.

They understood our specification document.

We created milestones and roadmaps together, and off they went building.

We had weekly project meetings.

And in what seemed like no time, we had the front end of our software, complete with the diagnostic and scoring function.

A business owner would be able to know exactly where their business was at, good, bad or ugly.

And all in a short time frame of less than 20 minutes … and they would know what they must go to work on right now in order to improve the building and running of their business.

The downside … all the "missions" (as we called them) that they had to do, were in rough paper format.

And so, we still had to talk people through what they needed to do and create tools and templates for them as we went.

But that was OK, because we were building what they needed as they needed it and we were able to fix up things that didn't make sense as we went.

We progressed to using a chat-box and serving up what people needed in canned responses, in a similar fashion to how we intended things to work in the future.

There was a problem, however. People had 24/7 access. And we were the chat bots … Hahahaha.

We needed to sleep as well, so, in 2018 we hired our first full time employee.

Up until then, all our team had been university interns, for periods of 3 or 6 months at a time.

And as it turned out this full-time employee we hired was no ordinary human being.

In the last 23 years I've had two absolute standout hires … and Agata was one of them.

She was a machine. She took ownership of everything in her job description and then everything else in between that needed to be done. With her help we hired a 24/7 team to handle the chat-box.

Which meant we could get back to fine tuning the "missions", tools and templates.

And in Easter of 2018, we hung up our ActionCOACH Franchise boots all together, going all in on Biznostics.

Things were about to get interesting … more so that we thought.

It All Goes Wrong

Now that we were all in on Biznostics … the only income we had was coming in was from our subscription clients … no more coaching clients.

Which meant a massive pay cut personally … ouch.

We had a bank of cash to keep developing the software, so there was that.

And we were all set to go off to Hong Kong in June 2018 to some massive Tech-Fest, where we were going to pitch our backsides off and find the investors, we needed to go global.

Okay, so, we had a lot of confidence and belief … what could go wrong.

Well roughly 2 weeks before the Hong Kong trip on the 4th of June 2018 … a public holiday … I went surfing.

It was an overcast day, and the ocean was messy and kind of all over the shop … but there was surf.

I should have known something was off that day.

20 minutes into the session, my surfboard narrowly missed stabbing me in the eye.

I should have gone in then, because that sort of thing just doesn't happen to me in the surf.

Half an hour later … I snapped a fin, clean out of the fin box. I should have gone home.

But no, my mate Mal lends me one of his boards and I keep surfing.

I'm racing along a wave at break-neck speed … I go to smash the lip

… anticipating that spray will go everywhere.

But instead … some back wash come through at that exact moment that I am hitting the lip of the wave.

And forces my board violently against my front foot … snapping pretty much every bone across the middle of my left foot.

Some bloke helps me out of the water … and then it's an ambo ride and a green whistle (that part was good).

Life can get in the way of the best laid plans.

I'm now in hospital for 10-11 days waiting for the swelling to go down before they can do the surgery.

I used the time in hospital to work on the missions, edit

them, fine tuning them, going through each and every one with a fine-tooth comb.

I had been believing for a miraculous healing before the surgery, therefore not needing surgery.

But that did not happen, I must confess I was pretty bummed about that.

So off to surgery I go. 5 hours of surgery done masterfully by one of the best orthopaedic surgeons in Australia.

But there's a problem, the pain blocker didn't work ... so when I came to, I was in a world of pain like I have never experienced before.

So much so, that I couldn't breathe and almost die ... I know right!!!

Then the bad news starts piling up.

You will never run again, one doctor says, seeing my Ironman shirt – joy killer!

Another doctor says, don't get your hopes up about surfing again – negative nelly!!

And then I ask the surgeon, what are the chances of me flying to Hong Kong?

NO CHANCE mate!!!!

But this was going to be our big break ... What is going on????

Too Confident

So, there was no Hong Kong trip for Gav … instead Rueben and Agata go off to Hong Kong to wow and dazzle the would-be investors.

And for me … not one moment in Hospital was wasted.

I used every minute I could to critique every mission, every tool and every template … to make sure everything was exactly as it should be for the next iteration of the platform.

Meanwhile … in Hong Kong, the team were pitching to everyone they could.

And they happened to meet up with a guy that Rueben and I both knew (not intimately, but we knew him), and he was very interested in our platform.

Very interested in fact.

So, he flew to Perth, and we went out for dinner, me on a kneel chair … discussing all sorts of things and all sorts of options relating to the platform, investing and shareholding.

It was looking like a $2M investment was imminent … all

the right noises were being made.

We drafted up a heads of agreement, and it was to everyone's satisfaction.

Now we should have waited until the money was in the bank.

But we didn't. Instead, we went off like a rocket, hiring the best people we could get.

In no time flat we had an A-class team.

From business development, to marketing, to finances, to software developers and everything in between.

We even borrowed money … a lot of money … short term we thought (we really did believe that), while we were waiting for the investment money to come through.

Why? Two reasons, absolute confidence and belief … and the dude said he was IN.

Neither of which are good enough reasons … EVER!!!! (just saying).

Turns out he had a few hiccups his end … unexpected and outside of his control.

Ummmm … Houston, we have a problem.

Problems are ok, in and of themselves, but when you cause them and aid them … well that just sucks.

So now we are absolutely scrambling to stay alive ... our cash outflows were completely ridiculous compared to our cash inflows.

It was time to make some hard decisions.

Some advice we received was to liquidate the whole thing and start again with the source code.

But that sort of caper just doesn't fly with someone like me.

Particularly when I know the people that I owe money to.

No! We had to own what was going on and we had to make it work and make it right.

It was time to prune this thing right back and with the help of our Accountant, both advice wise and financially, we did that.

And I have to tell you ... nothing sucks more than letting your whole team go, just before Christmas ... I felt sick to the core for weeks. I had completely and utterly let them and their families down.

We took a massive pay cut in order to help the business survive ... we were now on $300 a week each.

Our amazing city office was gone ... we were back to working from home and over zoom.

There was an upside, the software was in perfect working order and so stable, we didn't need any tech support. All thanks to the master "Chris" who made it so.

And we had very supportive lenders and creditors … which enabled us to get our outgoings down low enough to match our income, with a small surplus. (Extremely small).

It was now January 2019 and somehow, we had survived.

We were $2M deep into developing Biznostics … and still had close to a million in debts outstanding.

Where to from here? Was the burning question.

Trying to Salvage Things

During the early stages of developing Biznostics, one of our advisors had to said to us.

You realise that the worst possible scenario with what you are building is that you'll end up with better coaching tools.

At the time he said that; I did not want that to be true.

Yet here we were in the aftermath of all that had happened in 2018

… and it seemed he may be right.

So, we started to use the Biznostics platform as a support tool for our clients, keeping them accountable to doing what they must do, so that the fundamentals were in place in the business.

We had 1-2-1 clients, and we had small groups going … and the business was slowly building.

We had partnerships in place with major trade associations and ran seminars for their members and offered special deals, which was all thanks to a lot of work our man Russell had done the year before.

I admit, I had this expectation that it was all just going take off now … I mean surely, hadn't we been through enough?

But it grew slowly …

So, we added a short course program to our repertoire … Chaos to Control … a 12 week course.

This seemed to be a hit and carried us through for a while.

At the tail end of 2019, I was down the beach one day, hanging out with the Lord, looking for inspiration … and then I had a deluge of information pouring into my head.

The complete outline, outcomes and curriculum for a new short course program … the Business Apprenticeship … helping people new to business learn the fundamentals from the outset … and use a fair portion of what was in Biznostics to do this.

I even cracked out a mind map for a book that would support this

… more on that later.

I had an opportunity to work with a bloke new to business … I worked with him one on one with all the content from the new course and modified things as we went.

I carried this on until we were ready to launch the group course for the Business Apprenticeship … which we did …

We got our first small group up and running. And then Covid hit.

This should have been a positive for our business.

We were 100% online. We were in the education space.

And while in that period we only lost one client and gained some more.

The gains were not outstanding … just ok.

Yes, we were growing … just not at the rate I desired (yes, I know, I am impatient).

I started to write the book - The Business Apprenticeship … slowly, probably because I wasn't convinced within myself that someone would want to buy or read a book that I wrote.

We got through 2020 … the business had grown … we had paid off some debt.

Things were moving bit by bit … but not fast enough for my liking.

2020 really aged me. Something had to change in 2021 … it just had too.

The Year I Never Wanted

There is a big part of me that doesn't really want to revisit this part of my story.

But here goes ... eeeeeek ...

On the 4th of January 2021, I was taking my youngest son to work.

Which is only about 900 meters up the road.

As I was going up the slight hill into his workplace, the car decided it would do some jolting type of bunny hop movements.

This could not be good, I thought.

So, straight off to the mechanic, who confirmed the gear box had gone into limp mode.

Well dang it mate, we only have one car.

Long story short, the gear box needs to be fully replaced for a small sum of 50% more than the car is worth?!?!

Yep.

Then 4 days later we have some major family problems.

I won't go into much of those details here, but it was extremely traumatic and involved the police, at the "Christians" house in the street.

Let me just to say, it was nothing we or you would ever expect to have happen to you… even if you had a wild imagination.

Especially as what we would describe ourselves as: "a good Christian" family … and yet it did.

There was some good news, however … a little silver lining.

I landed a big client through one of our Partners … and they were too big for our software to handle.

So, I found myself back in the 1-2-1 Coaching game. Was God re- directing me? (I did wonder about this a little).

I gotta say, that it felt great!!! Coaching and mentoring again.

Within 6 weeks, I helped them see a way to add an extra $180K to their bottom-line profit, with 3 little changes.

I know right … happy days for them … and it felt good.

With this taste fresh in my mouth, I decided to catch up with a past client/friend for a coffee.

As we were having coffee, shooting the breeze, I said, "hey Pete, I'm back coaching, if you know anyone thatneeds a coach, think of me".

He looks me dead in the eye and says, I know a guy. I'm like wow, who?

Me he said … hahaha.

So, we got started at it … and he is still a client right now (well he is more than a client tbh).

Through my coaching and his (and his teams) efforts … let's just say his business is doing pretty well as a result.

Sometimes you just need that outside perspective, someone to get you focused on what is truly important and to let go of (or stop doing) things that won't help you achieve your goals.

And so, it seemed, despite some of the personal troubles and dramas (which I haven't really touched on too much … because they were pretty hectic) … things were afoot.

Until the 2nd of August 2021 …

I pretty much have Monday's off … let's call it time away from the business [These days it is called my Pray Day - my time to be directed by God for the week].

I take that step back, mostly time alone with God … but sometimes with an earthly friend.

I had been for a surf at Avalon with my mate Andy.

We went to the coffee shop after and had a good catch up over life, family, business … and everything in between.

I was feeling good, very good. We had encouraged each other.

I was driving home … and I was about 3 kms from home and my little BMW decided to do some weird jolting and jumping movements.

Hmmm, I have experienced this before, I thought to myself. And I don't like where this is going.

So, my car is dead and in limp mode and stopped in my garage.

How could this be, two different cars, with similar problems within 7 months of each other … really???

I thought that this was bad!

It couldn't get worse, could it?

But it turned out that "worse" was a knock on the door the next day at 11:01am.

Two police officers.

(I'm crying as I'm typing this).

They tell me, "Your son Jacob passed away yesterday".

Noooooooooooooooooooooooo! This can't be right!!!

What????

How?

Why?

My world came crashing down.

My heart was shattered into a thousand pieces.

How do you tell your 3 sons that their brother is dead?

How do you tell the rest of the family?

What do you do? Nothing, I mean nothing prepares you for this.

This isn't real, how can it be?

In 2020 my son Jacob had picked up a FIFO job, doing underground mining in the Northen Territory.

His swing was 3 weeks on 3 weeks off and that suited his bushman lifestyle.

Then covid hit and he found himself quarantining for 2 of his 3 weeks off at home.

So, in June 2020 he moved to Darwin, so he could have his swings off to truly relax.

What we didn't know then ... was the catchup we had with him on the 11th of June 2020, before he left, would be the last time we would ever see him physically alive.

Now we did have a great hug and tell each other, "love you" (he was one of the best huggers I know).

So that was good.

On the 20th of August 2020, he called to let us know he was all settled into his new home in Darwin.

We shared some great stories about his love for cowboy boots and making flies for his freshwater fishing.

Sharing pizza dough recipes and maybe having kids one day.

My favourite part of the conversation was when he said, "when I have kids, I want to be a Dad like you were to me".

We spoke for 1 hour and 13 minutes on facetime.

I will treasure that call forever in my heart and the memories of it are embedded in my soul.

We didn't know this at the time, but that would be the last time we would ever hear his voice.

And 3 days later would be the last text we would ever receive from him.

To this day, we still don't know why he cut off communication with us. All we know is he did and there was nothing we could do about it.

Later we discovered that he had cut off all communication with everyone we knew ... except just one person.

His last 11 months and 10 days on planet earth are a mystery to us.

We don't know how he was doing.

Every effort to contact him came to nothing, radio silence so to speak.

All we know is that he had struggled with mental illness and the voices in his head for many, many years.

So, we were left, without a son and with a lot of questions … and with no one to fill in the blanks.

We had to go to Darwin. We had to at least see his body one last time.

A friend paid for our flights and the hire car.

Another friend paid for our accommodation. Next minute we were on a plane to Darwin.

Have you ever had a situation where you thought this has to be as bad as it gets?

Surprise. It was about to get worse!

We found out that something had gone down between Jacob and his De-facto.

And after that incident, Jacob took his life.

I don't hold any blame on her about this outcome.

Over the years Jacob had many attempts to take his own life prior to this.

But this woman was intent on not having us informed of his death, as it turns out.

Tried to get him cremated before we got there.

And then we found friends in the most unlikely places that helped us as best they could.

The lead detective, the funeral home and the coroner's office.

So we did get to see our son one last time, but to this day we have never received any of his ashes.

Now we don't know Jacob's De-facto. We don't know what went on in their relationship.

We don't know why she has done what she has done, and we hold no malice towards her. All we knew was we now had a big hole in our hearts.

Our Church helped us organise a memorial service for Jacob.

The building was packed … and we celebrated the life that was Jacob Alexander Bassett.

But where to from here?

Time Out

For several weeks after Jacob's death, I just couldn't work …
I was unable to think straight or clearly.

Thankfully, my clients and my business partner (Rueben)
were very understanding … which I appreciated more than
words could ever express.

Initially I took about 3 weeks off, somehow, I thought I
would be ok after that.

But I was wrong! When I went back to work all I could
manage was a few hours a week.

So, I decided I would only do what I really had to do and
nothing more … This was educational in itself.

Because it is interesting how busy we get in our business,
doing all sorts of things, almost caught up in a cycle of
busy-ness for the sake of business.

But what if we only did what was truly important? I mean
the utmost of importance.

However, the absolute truth of my situation was that I was

broken, which meant I could only do what I had to do.

Life had changed so dramatically and so traumatically that I just wasn't sure what was what.

I needed a distraction, or so I thought.

A mate of mine who runs a coaching company on the East Coast of Australia was looking to expand. So, I put my hand up to run seminars for him all over the state of Western Australia.

While presenting on stage is definitely right up there in my high skill sets … something was off with this venture.

Was it a distraction? Absolutely!

Was it what I should be doing? Turns out, no it wasn't something I should be doing.

The problem I discovered was that going through the grief process really does have you all at sea, and decision making is not usually that sound when you are in the thick of it.

By February 2022 (6 months after Jacob passed away) … I had lost all bar 2 of my clients.

This was not something I was used to as a Business Coach.

But two clients stuck with me and worked with me where I was at. And they are still with me today, as I am writing this.

I really appreciate Peter and Josh ... a lot.

So, I was left in a space pondering: "where is this all headed?"

Then a friend of mine who I rely on for spiritual counsel said, "Gavin, you need to rest".

Interestingly enough, I needed little convincing, so that's what I did.

Rested … while only doing what I had to do, with my 2 clients.

This space of rest and time out allowed me the opportunity to take one of my granddaughters to toddler gym every Wednesday morning.

Then we would hang out at the park and have lunch together … we would have some crazy conversations, as only you can with a 3 year old who has an extremely vivid imagination.

It was a beautiful time in my life, one which I will always treasure.

Here's the thing, even in dark valleys, the sun (Son) always finds a way to shine.

And while I was getting good at just resting, it became very clear to me that I needed to stand down from Biznostics.

Then around Easter 2022, I received a prophetic word from a Prophet I trust, that God was looking to separate me from Biznostics. To which initially I thought, ummm ok.

And shortly after that, I had a very clear vision of two huts that were right next to each other, almost wall to wall, on top of a mountain.

Then there was some seismic activity on the mountain and both huts started to fall down the mountain and the outcome of that wasn't pleasant.

Then I heard the Lord say, the separation is to happen … you can do this yourself or I will do it. It will go well for you if you do it.

Another God directed thing, and prompt obedience was required.

I was at peace within myself to leave everything with my business partner in that venture, Rueben.

The software, the content, the tools, the templates … the lot.

We still had a fair size debt, so I had to stay on as a director and continue to pay in my share of the money to service the debt, which I was 100% behind … but otherwise, I had laid Biznostics down and walked away from it.

So, there I was resting … healing … rejuvenating … and it was good. Very good.

I spent countless hours in worship and in silence … allowing the Lord to minister to me, so that I could function again.

I wrestled with my faith somewhat.

Not in a way of, "hey God, how could you let this happen".

But more in a way of deliberation.

Was all the effort of being faithful and faithfilled worth it …
or was being more nominal the way to go. Were my expectations in this life and of God too high??

And as I was contemplating these things, I came across a
Brandon Lake song, "Don't You Give Up On Me".

In essence, the song is from God to me (or from God to you,
if you like).

A song where God is saying, I get how tough this is on you,
but don't you give up on me.

I played that song several times a day, as if it was God
speaking to me. And I did this to remind myself not to give
up on God, no matter what.

And this led me to the process which unfolded next.

New Beginnings

So, in amongst all this down time, of sitting with God, of sitting in my own thoughts, of ups and downs … I made a decision to go on a mission to find myself again.

What I didn't realise was the old me was gone and would never be found again.

As I was on this discovery journey, around July 2022, I started to get enquiries to help people with certain aspects of their businesses

… mainly in training their managers.

In fact, there were 3 businesses around the same time, I knew the owners and I knew their businesses very well.

I call these 3 clients … my rescue package … they didn't know that

… but that's what they were to me.

They were exactly what I needed at that point in time. And hopefully, I was what they needed at that point in time.

Two of them are still clients to this day, so I must be doing something right.

So, on the 1st of September 2022, the first day of spring, I started my new business coaching and mentoring venture … Bmultiplied. A name the Lord gave me for my new business.

To be multiplied. Business multiplied … a new beginning.

A premium service where I would work very closely with business owners and some of their key managers to help multiply their profits … or so I thought.

Now I wasn't setting any records for my own business growth.

But maybe, just maybe, instead of me finding myself again, perhaps there was a Gavin 2.0 amongst all this poop that had happened over the years.

And with all this poop, there's gotta be a pony in there somewhere, right? (if you know, you know).

Now, I used to be a rock-solid stable bloke … but the rough time we had been having since 2015 had done a real number on me.

Consequently, I found myself getting messed up by things that used to be water off a duck's back. I mean, it didn't take much to knock me flat.

At the end of November 2022, I decided to use a new payment processor for my business, which turned out to be a very bad mistake.

And 25% of what was then my month's income got stuck in their system somewhere. As in, they had it and I did not, and they weren't releasing it, for reasons that just didn't make sense then or even now.

I needed that money. I mean, I really needed it. It was no small change for me at that time, because this money was supposed to kick start the marketing for my business.

And I can I tell you; I allowed this situation to completely mess me up … and I mean completely and utterly.

Now in the past, if something happened that I considered bad, I wouldn't dwell on the problem or the circumstances, at least not for very long, instead I would focus on the positive, find a solution and move forward.

But that part of me seemed to have completely disappeared … and so I spiralled for almost 2 months on this one.

Yep, over Christmas and everything.

WARNING - this is about to get dark (but know this, I am ok now, rest assured).

Here's the thing I found for me … when someone in your family takes their life, it completely messes with your rationale thought process.

For me, I even thought, well if he did it, maybe I should to.

And that's where I found myself … with those types of dark thoughts and having them regularly.

Sadly, I even picked a day to end things … because you've gotta plan right?

I had decided if things weren't looking a certain way for me by 31 January 2023, then I was out. I was signing off.

I did say to you it was dark!!!

Here's the interesting thing, I think, anyway. Nothing really improved by that date in my circumstance.

It certainly wasn't looking like the way that I had decreed it should be!

Even that money that went missing was still missing from my business.

But on the 15th of January 2023, something inside me had changed

… I had hope again for the future.

Which is interesting, because I had not even recognised that it was hope that was absent, but it was.

Yet on that day, while in Church, God did a number on me.

The worship leader on that day, Gabby, was speaking about the power of the name of Jesus. So, I closed my eyes and started speaking the name of Jesus over my life and my circumstances … and right there in that moment, I had a vision.

I saw myself in a prison cell, there was a small amount of light coming in. And as I was believing in the power of the name of Jesus, as I was declaring the power of the name of Jesus … the prison cell broke down, wall by wall, and I was free.

Then I heard the Lord say, "who the son sets free is free indeed".

At the close of the message that day, our Pastor (Jemima Varughese) said that she had in mind 3 types of people as she was preaching. The first, she said, was people who felt like they were in prison, but there was some light and belief had not left.

God had me in mind that day. I mattered that much to him. And I am so very grateful.

From that day on, hope that had seemed lost and very absent … started to return.

And little by little (way too slowly for me), I started to become more aware of what Gavin 2.0 was going to look like … and what it couldn't be like … and my business started to grow.

Then something equally interesting happened.

My best friend Mal went to Japan with his family.

And when he came back, he told me this story he had heard while he was there … a story that absolutely resonated with me.

The story was about "Kintsugi" … the repairing of broken pottery with gold, silver, or platinum.

The philosophy behind it is to treat the break and repair as part of the history, rather than to disguise the brokenness.

And in fact, making the broken pottery more special and more precious than it ever was before.

It was time to allow God to "Kintsugi" me … and use my brokenness to make me better, stronger and more special than before.

So, Gavin 2.0 was being birthed … owning and loving my brokenness for who I had now become and could become.

And as this was taking place, around Easter 2023, I get a call from Rueben about Biznostics.

What could this be?

Back in the Game

Rueben had received a call from Karl, who we had known pretty well through our Partnership days between Biznostics and the Master Builders Association a number of years earlier.

Karl had since moved to an organisation that was supporting Aboriginal tourism related businesses around the state of Western Australia ... WAITOC - Western Australian Indigenous Tourism Operators Council.

Rueben and Karl had been speaking for quite a number of weeks about how WAITOC could benefit from either Biznostics or its content.

Rueben wanted me at the next meeting because of the significant role I had played in building the software and its functionality (I am not a software coding guy, let me clear on that).

I was like, "Lord, what is this about, I thought I was out of this whole Biznostics thing? I laid this down ... remember? Because you asked me to ... remember"?

Can I say, this troubled me deeply that I was potentially picking up something that the Lord had told me to lay down.

So, on that Sunday morning at Church, I went forward for prayer with Pastor Phil.

I told him my dilemma and as he was praying for me, he had a vision of me being on the bench in a sporting game and the coach was calling me back onto the field … back into the game.

Perhaps God was testing my obedience. Perhaps he was testing me out to see if the business had me or if he had me. I'm not really sure!

I just know he told me to lay it down, I did, and now he was sending me back onto the field.

So, I prayed, Lord, if I'm going to go to this meeting, you need to guide the conversation that comes out of my lips in this meeting.

The meeting was great … and it seemed I was back on team Biznostics (which I didn't see coming).

Karl had a project he had to deliver … providing business education, online to his members throughout the vast state of Western Australia.

And it became very clear, very quickly in that meeting … that we could repurpose Biznostics to meet the needs of his organisation … and white label it, so it was their version, not ours.

Dealing with Karl and his team has been some of the most in-flow business I have ever done in my life.

And over the course of a couple of months, we worked out an MOU that was pretty straight forward.

We were all on the same page, working for a common cause.

In the background we started interviewing software companies to help us achieve what we needed to change, so it was fit for purpose.

Fortunately, we found the right team, right here in our local city of Perth … which was awesome.

And in amongst all this, I was slowly but surely growing my coaching business.

But things were about to change up a notch … my assignment was about to be seriously activated.

Unlocking a Gift

A mate of mine (Matt "the legend" Ridley) had referred a business to me a few times ... and on go number three ... we finally met.

God's perfect timing ...

The couple who owned this business were (are) amazing ... and they helped unlock something in me, that had always existed, but outside of business, and never while I was doing business.

This next bit may sound like some kind of woo woo ... however, it is genuine and real, and it happens (and happens a lot).

Up until this point in time, when I started working with a client, I would get them to complete a thorough assessment of their business.

This was so that I would know exactly what I was dealing with, and they would know exactly where they were at.

This assessment had been built over many, many years,

using all my experiences and data from thousands of businesses I had worked with in some capacity.

However, when I left their business that first time after meeting them, I distinctively heard God say, forget your assessment ... they have these 2 key problems that they need to deal with and deal with now.

I'm like ... ummmm ... what? Really?

You know how I roll Lord ... my assessment thing, my structure thing, ya know ... nope the Lord, he aint buying it.

So, I tell them these 2 things ... and it's like they have known this all along but just haven't addressed it.

And this is the confirmation they seemed to need in order to deal with these things.

What's interesting is that both these things would have come out through the assessment, but they would not have had the priority the Lord gave them. It's like He knows stuff, hahahaha.

After this happened with them ... it continued to happen with other clients I was working with and even some businesses I wasn't yet working with.

In fact, at a business breakfast the next day, it happened twice. A breakfast I had been to so many times over the years (and this had never happened there before).

It was kinda cool … and kinda scary … and it was way outside my comfort zone (apparently this is called faith).

But I worked with it and still am … and it's actually amazing and still scary. The right word for this is probably more reverence than scary.

A prophetic gift for the marketplace from above had been activated … like a 6th sense! [Know this however, the power is not in the gift! It is in God, the giver of the gift!]

At about that same time, I had created an annual planning workshop for my clients.

And then I felt very strongly to offer this same workshop to a group I was part of in Mandurah, called KI (Kingdom Initiatives)

… for free … and to do it without expectation.

That's hard for a guy with high expectations …

So, the first weekend of July 2023, that's what I did … helped 15 people create their long-term dreams for their businesses and plan out their next 12 months.

This was followed by a similar group to ours that operated in Illinois USA, with 25+ people … but online this time.

At the time, I truly did not know where this was leading … I just knew that I felt alive again … I was making a difference … doing what I was supposed to be doing and the prophetic was flowing.

My business started to grow, with the types of businesses and people I have found that I truly love to help and work with - Kingdom Builders.

People eager to learn and grow, who want their businesses to grow, who will do what it takes … so that they can help others in their communities through their profits and success of their business.

A Kingdom side to my business was being unlocked and activated, even though I was not fully aware that's what God was up to.

When things are growing, good things are happening … and something really good was about to happen next.

Fun and Hard Work

The second half of 2023 was going to be interesting and exciting.

After enduring so much hardship, pain and grief in our family, the sun was now starting to shine through the clouds.

In the first weekend of August, what had become a time of grief for me and my family … was also going to be a time of joy.

My oldest son, Connor, married the love of his life. And we gained an amazing daughter-in-law.

On the business front, I had my diary set out.

It was clear when my Bmultiplied days were and when my Biznostics days were going to be.

And now it was time to get to work … repurposing Biznostics to meet WAITOCs needs …

This was to be amongst trips to Malaysia and the Gold Coast, and with Rueben away in Europe for 3 weeks.

We had legal agreements to sort out for WAITOC. Thank goodness for good lawyers with common sense.

Software development contracts to be sorted out, again so blessed to have a local team on hand.

We had to bring all of our content into alignment and into a consistent format, which turned out to be a bigger job than expected.

There was reviewing, editing, video reshooting, and re-shooting and more reshooting. And reviewing and editing (yes, I repeated that).

And all of that all over again and again.

So, suddenly, I was working 15 hour days, 6 days a week … fitting my coaching and mentoring into the spaces and gaps.

This was not the plan … What had happened?

This was crazier and more time-consuming than I had envisaged.

Rueben and I were getting the content right. The software people were getting the software right … and then duplicating it.

Then we were testing it … and they were fixing any bugs that came up.

Why does software have bugs?? Who decided that was the name? So many bugs …

And so, the cycle went on and on.

Until … boom … the white label version of Biznostics … the WAITOC online business education platform was ready.

So now it was time to onboard their advisors, so that they could serve their 250+ members.

This was a great milestone for WAITOC and a great milestone for Biznostics.

It was great for me … because I could breathe again.

And at this same time, we welcomed grand-daughter #3 into the world … Malia "more joy" Bassett, a beautiful little cherub, I don't mind saying.

So, heading into Christmas 2023, was way different to 2022, let me say again, way different … thank you God.

I had been adding more clients to my business (and I hadn't even noticed a common theme yet) and my coaching and mentoring business was now stable.

I had a great crew of clients … only one didn't fit the mould, and they were on hold never to return, it is good how some things work out.

And I could firmly say … **I am grateful for my life** … something I had not been able to say for quite some time.

It was in this fun time and hard work time that God had been up to something in my business and in me, something I had not been noticing.

But it would soon be obvious ...

Stable

I was finally back in a place where I was stable personally and consequently, my business was also stable.

It is interesting how your business will reflect where you are at.

Which means there is something to the Proverb – as a man thinks so he is.

The Lord was kind enough to add 2 more Kingdom Builders to my client base.

Not just any type of client, I was attracting Kingdom Builders … the Lord was trying to highlight something to me … but I still wasn't noticing it, hahahaha.

Not only was this great financially, but it also started to shape where my business would eventually head … even though I was not that cognisant of this at the time.

As Christmas 2023 drew near, I had other client opportunities that seemed to come out of nowhere … some excited me, others not as much.

Suffice to say, none of them came off in the end. Which confused me at the time, but now I see why.

One of the opportunities shaped my framework of what I don't want … the other caused me to create something which is now core to my service offering to this day.

Something I have learned … if I allow God, He will use everything to my advantage.

Which is in essence what Romans 8:28 says.

And so, as I looked back on all that had happened in my entire life

… I saw how God was using every single ingredient. The things I thought were good.

The things I thought were bad. And all the other stuff in between.

God's ways are not my ways and His thoughts not my thoughts.

Which meant He could use everything to equip me, the way I have been equipped.

And he could use everything that has happened and the way it has happened to bring me to this point in time to use me how He wants to use me

So, here I was …stable … and ready.

A convergence was occurring … where everything that had happened in my life was coming together all at the same time.

It was His design in making me assignment ready.

The Convergence

I have always been very purposeful the whole time I have been in business …

In fact, I think I have been that way ever since I got into the workforce way back in 1987.

I don't say this to brag … it's just purpose is talked about a lot out there.

In the last couple of years, I've been on a journey to really dial in my assignment.

Unlocking it … to activate it.

It's crazy to think, that all my life experiences and business experiences have been converging.

For such a time as this.

And yet they have been.

I must confess that since starting Bmultiplied, I knew something would be quite different this time.

I didn't know what, but everything within me really wanted

to know what that would be.

And the answer seemed to allude me.

Even my spiritual advisor, Michelle, told me … "this will not be like what you've done before".

I mean I heard what she said, but at the time I couldn't quite comprehend what that meant.

So, I started leaning in, pressing in. I was asking, seeking, knocking.

Yet one thing I've learned, the timing is never mine. It's his!

There were clues being dropped.

And apparently, I can be slow on the uptake at times. But once I get it … I'm away … it's acceleration time.

And he knows that too, so he's careful what he lets me know and when (hahahaha).

As I mentioned earlier, the first clue was dropped in May 2023. And I knew it was something.

I could sense it and feel it. But it still wasn't clear to me.

And by no accident, I have found myself, little by little, working with more clients who have an assignment.

I found myself teaching things that I was discovering about assignment.

More clues …

But it took getting out of the country for a week. Getting away from everything I know.

Being out of my comfort zone.

With a bloke who really knows what he's on about, when it comes to helping you really dial in who you should be working with.

My mentor James.

So, the penny finally dropped for me.

Which is probably why I found myself in a place of excitement and a genuine nervousness.

Things were about to change. It was time for a shakeup.

It was time to birth the "Kingdom Assignment Movement".

To help fulfil my calling on this planet by God to advance His Kingdom here on earth.

And in doing so, I have found, at least for myself, my assignment is not my purpose.

However, my assignment has purpose.

The purpose is to change something, to shift something … to bring an abundance of goodness, life and love in a way that glorifies God and highlights His Kingdom here on earth.

It may sound like I'm being pedantic … perhaps … but I don't think so.

Yes, be purposeful in all you do. Please!

But when you unlock, activate, and pursue your assignment.

When you become sold out for that, you discover this is so much bigger than you.

It's not even for you … it is for God and it's for others.

So, for me, instead of finding my purpose and feeling good about myself … "complete" if you will.

I'm pursuing my assignment, to complete what I was born to do on this planet.

This isn't about me and there will be a cost, as there already has been.

And I am pretty convinced most people wouldn't sign up for what I have had to endure to get to this point that I am at.

Here at the place where I am all about my assignment.

That's why I started the Kingdom Assignment Movement in May 2024 … to help instigate 1,000,000 Kingdom Assignments on this planet.

It's funny, I set the target at 1,000 in my lifetime.

Then God added 3 zeros … and said, remember, this isn't

about what you can do.

It's what you will allow me to do through you, He said.

Am I terrified about how this will and can work ... YES!
Am I excited about the journey ahead ... also YES!

For me personally, everything that has ever happened in my life and business has converged for such a time as this.

I'm pursuing my assignment with all my heart ...

The Assignment of Kings

And so, on this journey I have discovered that I am a King and Priest in the marketplace for God and His Kingdom.

My ministry is not inside the 4 walls … it is out there in the marketplace.

Here's an interesting biblical fact … most of the miracles Jesus did were in the marketplace … not inside the temple.

And here is what I know is true for me and for you.

I was born specifically in this time to do what he had pre-ordained me to do.

He has seen everything that I would do, He wrote it all down in His book even before I was born.

He allowed the things of life to mould me, shape me, and break me, so that I could be used for His purposes.

He is calling more and more of His Kings in the marketplace to unlock, activate and pursue their assignments.

My hope is that my story inspires you to get into a place

where you go all out to pursue your assignment.

I sincerely hope that you won't need to go through everything that I have gone through.

But I know that God does not waste one drop of all that has happened in your life.

He perfects it to be useful for His Kingdom ... if you will allow it and if you will say Yes to him.

It is time for the Assignment of Kings.

It is time for you to unlock, activate and pursue your assignment. If I can help in any way ... reach out to me and let me know.

God bless you.

Gavin Bassett
Kingdom Assignment Movement

To find out more about the Kingdom Assignment Movement:

- Got to the Website: www.bmultiplied.com.au

- Join the Assignment Bite List: admin@bmultiplied.com.au

www.ingramcontent.com/pod-product-compliance
Lightning Source LLC
Chambersburg PA
CBHW050823090426
42738CB00020B/3463